In The WHALE

Leonard Wallace Robinson

First Printing

ISBN: 0-935306-21-8
Library of Congress Catalog Card Number: 83-70061

Acknowledgment is gratefully made of the publications in which these poems first appeared: "In the Whale" in *The New Yorker*; "Squalor and Early Sorrow," "Cement, Etc." in *New Letters*; "On the Edge" as "the edge is always there" in *The Hampden-Sydney Review*; "Priestess," "To Market" in *The Chowder Review*; "Yes" in *Cutbank*; "Hard Questions to Some Animals, With Answers," "In the Window of Knowing," "Near Damascus," "Ode to Light" in *Studia Mystica*; "Anger, Long Tempered, Years Later," "Curator's Son and Poet at the Piraeus," "Wonder" in *The View from the Top of the Mountain* (anthology, Barnwood Press).

Publication of this book was assisted by a grant from the National Endowment for the Arts.

Cover art: Jonah Asleep and the Whale, sarcophagus fragment, Louvre, from a photograph in *Early Christian Art*, ed. Pierre Bourguet, William Morrow and Company.

Design by Barbara LaRue King

The Barnwood Press Cooperative
Rt 2 Box 11C
Daleville, IN 47334

Printed in The United States of America.

For my beloved Patricia

Contents

Three: Back Ways In

Prelude

In the Whale

In my turquoise sweater, disgruntled
that I was so late, I left my house
in Mexico this morning and stepped
into a crystal light and was caught
like a blue plum in bright sugar
water, caught in open sunlight, but
down the street under the shade of
that great tree by the underground
water, the river that feeds our town,
was a boy much farther along toward
total saturation than me; he was in
a sharp brown-green condition, the
razor light limning him (God alone
knows how through all that shade)
still as a stone against the cheviot
wall, his back and right foot up,
supporting him, his peaked cap in
that actinic rain drenched in mottled
clarities. And just behind him in
full sun, like me, a Mexican woman in
a blue rebozo, with a basket of tomatoes
on her head, overfull, plunges down
the hilly path full tilt right into
the shade and turns into slow-motion
damson-blue with light coming through
and strawberry top, and then a white
dog is sucked into the emulsion, gives
up, lies down, and now I, electrified,
magnetic, am drawn over into the jellied
shade, plunge in, and sun surrounds and
shade engulfs all four and now we hang
all motionless together in this morning
miracle, leviathan, force field of grace.

One: On the Edge

Pasión/Industrial/Mexicana

I am in love in a certain sense
with a Mexican washerwoman in that
line of sixty public washtubs, the
clean-lined woman, very dark, with the ponytail

and white dancing earrings. I gave her those
jade earrings surreptitiously and she
looked at me with such wonder I
thought I would die. Her eyes misted over

and her mouth softened and she looked
down and away and took them.
She has five children all beautiful and
her husband looks like the dean of men

at Bowdoin. He's an unemployed glazier. She dresses
him in loose-weave cardigans, blue linen pants
that fit perfectly, and gray moleskin shoes.
Above their one-room adobe hovel here at the edge

of town their television antenna gleams
in the tropic sun, the only one, a crown. She
dresses her five children like fashion models
in yellow sunsuits, patent leather shoes, etc. and

cuts their hair highstyle herself. The boys look
vaguely New England, sun-browned. I am a father and I
understand her but how does she do it? Know style? Get
the money? She looks at me so wistfully. Her needs

drive me crazy. I can see each one of them in her
upper lip and in those huge eyes that look away from
me almost angrily saying, what's the use, no chance
no chance — for her anyhow. She is putting her needs

outside her, I think, putting them on the
children, each a beautiful new blue lottery
ticket. She had them when passion seemed the same
to her as her ambition. I have never

seen a mouth so beautiful as hers. Even as a bone-
poor man I had not the faintest idea
that wanting could be so built-in to one,
the hungry mouth the lovely one.

Rich Men

Rich men have duck blinds and great
hunting coats full of racks of bullets.
Their long guns with carved stocks
and incised barrels smoke in the early
mornings from the action versus ducks
near Plymouth or Gloucester, Mass. They never
tire. They are all trained by experts
in everything and can beat you at anything
you pride yourself in: running, swimming, boxing.

They have light skin that glows and slender
legs and they have blond hair along
their legs and on their forearms. They have
a curious disregard for their own safety
and never worry about their health. They run
the far-off things like polo matches and
sailing regattas and they run the national government
and war almost perfectly.

They are warm and complex. They live on or
near the sea in beautiful isolation loving
their long sleek boats and wives. They plan
their leisure with 18th century care, devising
fascinating parlor games or suddenly going on
terribly wild binges, revels that would inflame
your deepest venery if you should learn
the details. If, during one of these revels, they come
to visit you, it is because they want your sister.

On the Edge

That Spanish gentleman there is showing his handyman what remains to be done on the new hotel the Spanish gentleman will never finish, pointing upward with his ruby-ringed little finger so delicately and waving his hand in a rubbing-out gesture while his young handyman, almost as Spanish-looking as the gentleman, nods yes, then really sees what's being shown and nods again, yes, while his beautiful wife watches them, looking at them sideways from the broom she's pretending to sweep in front of their white hut with. She is swift and furtive as a sparrow bobbing in a seeded furrow. What is the bright white shirt of the gentleman made of? It is so white. Is his profound courtesy more than skin deep? Does the nodding yes of the handyman express gratitude and a willing dependence on his *patrón*, as it seems to? Could his yes-saying be allied to an inner goodness and not just be high policy?

The handyman and his beautiful wife have seven children and she is even more Spanish-looking than he is, almost Irish-looking in fact, with freckles alongside her nose and great purple eyes. They live in the adobe hut, of course, but it is owned by the *patrón;* it has two rooms and is windowless like all the others, but has a good cement roof against the rains that are coming soon. The *patrón* has seen to the roof.

But perhaps the handyman is in a rage against his *patrón* because he will not help him to develop his single talent, as a cook, that has vaguely stirred in him from time to time but with no evident strength or stability. Does the handyman really wish to become an independent human being? Would a vocation really give it to him? He plays basketball beautifully on the public court, dresses in a dark blue golf shirt with white piping around the collar, chinos with egg-and-dart cuffs and adidas with blue hearts around the rims of the soles. But listen to the ground here. Are these edges, jumping-off places? Listen to the birds; static; to the handyman; static, devotion to speed, devotion to scoring from deep center, a dimness.

Now, look into the wife's eyes. They are terrifying. She is certainly ready, on a verge, ready for anything. In her back yard, over the cold water tub she scrubs with a cold water bleach as corrosive as lime; through the tree over the tub the sun swoops down on her like a swan; her red hands smoke with their practiced swiftness in the water; she ignores their weeping; the social security doctor calls the pains in her hands degenerative arthritis. But names will never help her. The pains are the cause of her dreadful hurry, the first sign of a terrible coldness that is beginning on the edge, in her touch. Hurry! Yes, for it will grow till she is monstrous with resignation. Will the *patrón* be able to help her? At least in some way that has not yet become clear to him despite the strange enormous whiteness of his shirts, his frightening courtesy?

Squalor and Early Sorrow

I was sitting in a kerosene-stove-heated bar
in Hoboken with my girl who loved squalor and
the ex-mayor asked me to put him up in a flop-house
for the night, and later, because I couldn't afford
that he asked me for just another drink and told me
he had learned (in Greece) exactly how
to control the Jersey mosquito who made life
such a terrible misery in that state but I couldn't
pry the secret out of him for three more drinks
on me but when he was ready and willing to talk
he couldn't. She and I went home on the 2 A.M.
ferry and sang so beautifully together on the bow
you'd swear that only love could make such harmony,
but no, she really loved squalor not me who could
only locate it for her and she went off soon after
with a guy she said was a labor leader and I learned
he beat her nearly to death three times when drunk
before she left him for good. Good? Did I say for Good?
Not for her I'll bet. Never, nice and beautiful as she was.

furn.rm.   riv.vu

good boys alone as wolves
live in   furn.rms.
along the   black riv.   eat
alone in all-nite   EATS

break.   din.   sup.   fight off
strangers   weird needs   wants   go
each alone to   fites   flicks   f'ball
games and howl with the fans.

no pa   no home   no
sis   no ma   no bro.   no
relig.   no dough   no girl   no
friend   no bus.   no fut.   no

telef. even to be foned up
on   watch telev.   and
      the snaky riv.   the black
shallows howl. they dream

of running close together in the
dark   each pair of cold eyes
lit up with   ma-moon   all
bros.   one bus.   one fut.   one fam.

The Provincetown Boat

I stand in a dark blue soft-flannel overcoat and a dark blue fedora hat and in shiny black shoes by the sea. The tide is starting to come in, the small waves approaching my black shoes in frills, like thrown feather boas, like young girls coming close and then going back in shrill retreat; but each time they get quieter and bolder. The seagulls float overhead, enormous, over-fed from the town dump, appetite for fish almost gone entirely, barely able to dive; one huge one, fat and stuporous as a Goodyear balloon, is just a few feet over my head, hanging there. This great bird shits on my blue fedora.

"Hey mister," shouts one of three tall boys. All three are thick-legged, thick torsoed; I'd noted them long before when they were mere dots on the otherwise empty curve of the sea edge, and I had watched them surreptitiously, out of the corner of my eyes, as they approached. I'd known at once they spelt trouble. "Hey mister," the same voice says again when I do not respond. They are about thirty yards away, directly behind me. "Dincha know Fatso shatso on you?" he asks scornfully.

I look out to sea. The Boston-Provincetown Boat is coming out of Provincetown. But they stopped that boat in 1940, or 1930 or 1950. I'm certain of that.

"Hey mister," shouts a deeper voice, quite deep, from the three. "You like bird shit on your hat?"

I should turn around of course. My father used to turn on trouble and look it right in the eye. But I can't make myself turn the way he did. Never could. I should smile and wave and nod thanking them. Then I should take my hat off, look at the white smelly lime on its crown, its rich blue crown, make a rueful funny face at the three boys, eyebrows up, mouth half open in mock-astonishment, then grin at them and take my handkerchief out ostentatiously and wipe the shit off. But I can't turn around. I can't start the action.

"Hey dumb-dumb" — it's the deep voice again — "you deaf or something?" I knew they'd stopped to watch me. I knew their voices would become hostile. They were bristling at my lack of response.

The Boston-Provincetown Boat with its gleaming white hull was well off the Point now. Glad they were renewing that service; a marvelous ride, past Ocean Bluff, Fieldstone, Sea View, Scituate, Said, Quincy, K'If, Hanover-Four-Corners, etc. Three hours and two minutes to Rowe's Wharf in Boston. I'd gone once with my oldest brother when I was eleven and he was twenty-five. Could barely remember it. Caught sight of my first pair of breasts in an inside cabin porthole; wonderful; like two small white birds with red tufts; it colored my whole feeling about the Line (Red Star? White Star? Soft Star? Can't recall.) for the rest of my life. Small things like that (two of them) can be so decisive.

While I'd distracted myself in this manner the small frills of incoming tide finally overcome their shyness and rush in before they can change their minds and get my shiny black shoes right where they live, right over the tops; in fact they get me right up to my ankles, over the bottoms of my dark pinstripe pants.

"Hey, Jesus Christ, look at that!" It's the third voice, soprano, a hysterical voice. "Something's wrong with that guy. He's just standing there. He don't even get outa the way. Maybe he's nuts."

"Hey, dumb-dumb" says the first voice again. "Be honest. Are you nuts?"

"I think he's the suicide type," says the deep voice. "Let's rescue the son of a bitch."

"Right on," says the hysterical soprano.

I know they are starting toward me. But I still can't turn around. I try. I'll say that. I could wink and give them a broad grin. I could put my hand in my overcoat pocket and make believe I have a gun on them. But I can't make my hand do it. It's like one of those much-discussed dreams where you can't move. I look at the Boston-Provincetown Boat, two stacks, two white birds with the red-tipped tops. I take a step forward. Yes, I can move. But forward only. The three boys are coming up on me. I start boldly forward. Long strides into the drink. The water is shallow for a long way out. But finally I'm up to my middle and then more quickly up to my neck and I start to swim. Hard going of course; this hat, coat, suit, shoes. They don't make things easier. But I'm strong. And young. And have the motive and the cue. I head north-east by east. I'll come abreast of the white boat off about Scituate on this course, thirty miles dead ahead.

Praise for Clarissa Harlowe

What long-billed vermilion dawn-bird is it
Who moves in that red thicket with such exquisite
Caution, there where the strange bait lies; consulting; her red
Eugenie tuft up, front, down, up; her beautiful head
A blur to deceive a danger? The clear snare closes.
Can't she leave? She pulls. The horror rises
Like the day. Pulls. She cannot leave.
Pulls, tears, bites, tears again. The leg stays behind, a bleeding
Stump. The Hunter may weep. But the Hunter does not weep.
He has no heart. At all. And no sweet
Dawn-bird will he have, either. Not if she dies.
Not even if she lives (beautiful One-leg). Never.

Cement, Etc.

The narrow tar roads with those fat wormlike cement borders on either side painted white; they have them as the main roads in cemeteries, sanitariums, soldiers' homes and in New England preparatory schools. They always lead to empty administration buildings, deserted dining halls, padlocked toolsheds, far off solariums for the convalescent, secondary athletic fields and around deserted dormitories. Endless, no place to turn around, the eight-inch high cement shoulders just high enough to keep one on the narrow, turning tar roads. The paraplegics' sun parlors in the distance are too far to walk to ask directions of the men lying or sitting there. The wrong turn was certainly made way back there. The right road wouldn't go on and on like this. The small bent-over figure attending the sprinkler is too far away to ask and the grass is too soft to drive over, newly planted and spongy. Drive? There is no car. This is walking. But the new grass, sparse as the hair on a fontanel, isn't even for walking on.

Salvation! The figure in the long trench coat, a doctor or a teacher or alumnus, coming through that thick stand of beeches, with the smile . . . Oh, god, he's a bum. With the clown's red nose and heavy beard and now, up close, the smell of booze, and the coat is an ankle length polo coat, badly stained, blue wine stains, the cloth in parts threadbare. The coat has a sash belt stylish in the 'thirties; Dick Powell wore one in the Fox Movietone News newsreel when they took his footprint at Grauman's Chinese in wet cement, his little white foot peeping out from the polo coat like cream cheese, his face expressing some kind of pain as though it might be true what they said about him and Marion Davies and Hearst on Hearst's yacht, their secret about the man (people said) that Hearst caught with Marion and shot and dumped overboard. It was hard to explain Marion's and Dick's successes in the movies otherwise, if one considers their lack of talent. For millions those successes could only be the result of blackmail. The footprints of numberless other stars lie with Dick's now in the wormless cement at Grauman's Chinese if they haven't broken it up yet.

"You're *lost?*" the drunk in the ankle length polo coat says. "Let Jamie help." He reeks of old and new booze. The fly front of his polo coat is stiff with vomit. But he takes over, presses his body close, and holding on tight around the shoulder with a powerful grip he forces a staggering, three-legged-race trot, his closeness and strength vaguely erotic. But this is far from solving anything, getting located. No. That's a wrong conclusion. These are the movements of a knowledgeable person in a place he knows well. This *is* someplace all ready. Jamie smiles reassuringly, nods, and retires to a phone booth. Escape is now possible through streets of shining brass poles joined with velvet ropes used for peaceful crowds at parade grandstands, funerals, theatres, movie palaces waiting for the next show, etc.

But, shortly, choices must be made. The main street suddenly forks in two, goes this way and the other way and — ohhhhh. Thank god. Safety at last. Two policemen. Young, good natured; sympathetic. Tremendously so. One is blond and smiling; the other is black-haired, Irish as paddy's pig. And smiling too. The three are in a place like the World's Fair in Flushing Meadows, but deserted now; there are miles and miles of empty parking places marked with parking meters like high pewter headstones. "Oh, you're *lost.*" The blond policeman looks at his partner, his face eager, almost a cartoon of sympathy. "He's lost, Joe," the blond says to paddy's pig. Joe looks at his partner, his face, too, ablaze with interest, his eyes like enormous lamps. "Do you think we can help him?" Joe says. "Certain, *certain,* coz," says the blond. "All we need to solve is the problem of — ah — ahh — destination." "Reet, reet," Joe replies enthusiastically. "You've *nominated* it. Again. You never fail." The blond nods happily. "Well," he says, "we can now say for certain that he *and* his friend are both lost. Well, almost for certain." Joe smiles and says with emphasis: "They're both lost," nodding vigorously as at a discovery, and he looks toward the far off telephone booth where the bum is still talking.

"HE isn't a friend of mine!" the lost man says suddenly. "I just asked him a direction, is all." "Oh, says Joe, "*is all.* Oh, *is all"* and looks at the blond cop shaking his head, beaming. The blond hits his own head gently with his nightstick, his smile incandescent. *"Is all,"* he repeats. "A lost grammarian." Joe nods: "Did you ask him a direction before he comes jazzing up here hugging you," says Joe, "or did you ask him *after* he comes jazzing up here hugging you?" They look at each other, terribly pleased. "Before or after?" grins the blond cop as he taps the lost man gently on the head with his nightstick. Then they both start shuffling around the man in a dance, smiling and singing, "Before or after, before or after, before or after," tapping him on the head at each "after," at first gently, then, as they circle more swiftly, harder, almost imperceptibly harder, each time.

But, salvation again? A figure in a long trench coat is seen. In the middle distance. Doctor, teacher, alumnus? No. That's a long polo coat. The clown, finished telephoning, has clearly taken the situation in at a glance and now he comes running in an unsteady, blundering gallop across the half mile of unpeopled, netless tennis courts that separate them, calling, and signalling with his hands frantically as if he had a message for them; but his voice is barely heard in the distance, seems to be saying: "caw, caw, caw," gently as he races toward them. "Look!" says Joe in delighted amazement, leaving off the hitting dance and pointing with his nightstick. "Good heavens, Joe!" says the blond cop: "It's the U. S. *Horse* Marines," and he pokes his right ear with his nightstick and hums the Lone Ranger theme from William Tell softly. "I don't mind saying I'm scared badly, comrade," Joe says, grinning widely. He pauses, watching, for a moment. Then he says: "But you do see what's going to happen, don't you?" The blond nods: "It's too good to be true," he says excitedly and just as he does the clown's lumbering gallop changes to a series of astonishing slow-motion leaps. Joe bends over with laughter. "Oh, wonderful, wonderful," he says, tears streaming down his face, "He's hit it right in the middle." The blond turns to the lost man. "They just put it down this morning," he explains in a strangled soprano, pointing toward the clown. "Wet cement for — ten — new — tennis — courts." He doubles over. "The jackpot," Joe exclaims in the same laughing soprano; "it's like running in cream cheese." "Anything to make an impression," the blond cop says and he sinks to his knees, hitting the ground with his nightstick and the palm of his left hand alternately. At that moment the clown falls face forward into the cement and the moment he does the blond gets up and the two cops start toward him at once. "He'll be immortalized," Joe says. "Not just footprints, a whole body print." "And a life mask, to boot," says the blond. "Yeah, to boot," says Joe, and they both bend over with laughter as they move out.

When they have gone a few hundred yards or so the lost man sees a small crevasse of crumbling cement leading down to his left and he flees down into it. It leads to a huge white culvert or sewer conduit, a great pipe really. This leads out into a canyon, an ancient dry riverbed, its sides too steep for climbing. The canyon stretches away endlessly. But he has to go on. At least it's cool here, out of the sun and in this brisk breeze. In a way it feels like Wall Street, totally deserted on a windy Sunday morning, its dust blowing like sand along the valley between two endless dunes.

Three Postcards and
Three Lake Dreams

You ask about the weather. Splendid.
"Splendored," Mother says. To sum up,
Bertram, it's as peaceful as hell here.
A path of green grass leads to a green
lake. The white birds may be American
egrets. They sail head back, like clippers
with their royal gallants full. That's
about it.

The little girl's mouth is full of curses. They rail
out of her, lizards and scorpions, as she stands in front of
her red house on the soft edge of the lake. She can point
her mouth like a gun. She points it at Mother. One of
her lizards has wings. A scorpion stings her on the lip,
thank God.

Oh, yes, many colorful ceremonies during
the year, Bertram. Burial is by water, a kind
of flat-bottomed gondola with a burnished
silver prow bears the body, the oars are
muffled and relatives follow in black boats
to the Isola Di Cimitério, a square green jade
in the Lake covered with neon-blue grass. Real-
ly beautiful, Bertram. They use your bones
for commercial lime if the grave rent isn't
paid up right on time. But it isn't easy to
be buried here. There's hardly enough grave-
room for the rich, the very rich. Heat's be-
come terrific now, ninety-eight for ten days,
and of course Mother suffers from it. Both do.

The storms beat regular as breath, scorpions learn to do
the dead-man's float, a white roc circles, searching for
a sailor who has been lost for years, wandering among

the cast-iron benches on Telltale Island. How dines such
a man, on rodents, scorpions?

> If Rose Fandetti in the fourth grade could
> see me now, Bertram, at home in her own, her
> native land watching the white birds by the
> hour. The weather's splendored, as Mother
> tirelessly puts it. You could swim all year
> round here if the Lake were clean. It isn't.

You sail your small sloop past your youth but the jib
tears on the windless lake, shreds itself. On the star-
board rail a cardinal weeps for the newly dead.
Monstrous, a butterfly sings
from the small sextant.

two mothers

i pose myself against the cold city as against the cold universe and straighten my irish back and march straight in. the clock says 2 as clear as crystal. i say "double scotch" my voice a bell of sobriety, of clarity. slowly he shakes his head and his mouth forms a silent "no" and then another one as round as doom, as clear as a dancehall hostess to a sailor, then he leans over toward me. "you been in here twice in the last hour," he says. news to me. "what against me?" i say.

he smiles a little in spite of himself, like a glass balloon exploding, the same cop-smile you see in 3rd degree rooms, the quick smile and soft talk just before they break all your teeth with a big fist. "i got nuttin against you, mac, i like you is all," the bartender says to me. "you'll thank me tomorrow," his voice is like his waring blender for lady's drinks, like he eats gravel. "what makes you thin' i'm drunk?" i say. i stumble on that first "k" like on a step but i recover neat as a mountain goat on the second. "look at your hat," he says and stands aside so i can see in the mirror behind him. my hat's on sideways, the left side in front. i look like napoleon. "and where's your overcoat?" he says. "it's cold as a bastard out. you left your overcoat someplace. if i give you a drink you'll leave your suitcoat or maybe your godamn shoes someplace and you'll freeze to death," he says. "i ain't gonna be responsible."

i straighten my hat as he's talking and i say quietly, "you're a pricka misery, you know that?" but it's more a statement than a question. he gives me the same cop smile and shakes his head as though mystified. "you had your coat a half hour ago when you come in here," he says leaning closer to me as if confidentially across the bar; but i step back, out of reach of any ball bats behind this cute mother. oh yes, he keeps one behind his back often enough. guess why. "you probly left your coat at tim's," he says. "better go back and get it in case you did. he'll be closin' about now." i spit softly toward him in insult and go out backward while he shakes his head as if he's really mystified by me. him mystified.

but i get back to tim's just as he's closing the door and he's got
my coat over his arm and he says: "you're lucky, mac" and he
puts my coat over my head and squeezes my head. "lucky little
mac" he says. you wouldn't believe how big tim is. i feel like
an egg under a sofa pillow, just as helpless too and i squirm and
yell "you godamn mother," but he squeezes harder and says
laughing "you're a lucky little lush all right" and lets go and i
straighten out and put on my coat. "you'd a froze tonight," he
says. and i could feel a little how cold it was on my cheeks. he
shivers and hunches his shoulders and rubs his palms together
fast. "jesus," he says, "get home." he starts to close the door.
"you'll sleep," he says. "you've had enough to sleep. go on home
now, mac." his face is in the crack of the door for a last second
like when you're putting the dog out for the night and i spit softly
in his direction in insult. how the hell does he know if i've had
enough. he gives me that mystified smile bit and shakes his head
and then he closes the door and locks it.

The Dream

In the room of the two prisoners
A woman is wrapping a body in
Newspapers. The two prisoners are
Seated on a Louis Quinze Chaise

Longue. Their instructress is
Amusing in her running talk and
Yet informative, showing how it
Must be done. But I, the younger prisoner,

See blood is showing through the news-
Paper. The old prisoner is hopeless
And amused but I am horrified for
Now I know we're next. I bolt

And make the door but Medea, our
Instructress, makes it too and
I must take my seat again. I bolt
A second time, catching her off

Guard (a crucial moment with the
Butcher string half round the paper).
The front door is massive, oak
Carved in flowered clusters; it

Comes back slow, slow, and Med-
Ea is almost at me as I
Slip through, find myself on the
Great steps going down to freedom.

Two: Night Dreams

print

i have some time and the will and so
drive aimlessly, wandering through
my country, seeing it for the first
time really. i go south, north but always west.

and now i am inside a japanese
print in my friend's house in
high montana, looking out my
bedroom window through a scrim
of pinetree branchings to the top
of the fat gray-brown mountain
not a hundred yards away
lying like a smooth-flanked water-buffalo
on its side in the cold december sun
its sucking calves
hidden from sight by my high window sill.

these western hills are asian, animal, un-
american, connected to history in some
uncanny manner. great stretches
of the tetons and the little rockies
look like vast head-dresses of eagle feathers
stamped on ridges. and gallery on gallery
of granite figures, mongol faces in profile
sit or lie along the skylines, a patience
caught in stone. the mountains
waited for their people and they came.

the print i'm in is japanese all right.
the close by mountain has formal hillocks
colored like a tiger and it has a single
diagonal path with just one person on it,
in a black coat. high-cheeked, gold-
skinned, mongol-eyed they came across
the icelocked bering sea and down
splitting up at times, some staying
along the coast, some moving inland but

always travelling down; down mexico,
down peru, swift skilfull hunters,
fighting their terrors, losing every-
thing and starting each time again,
eyeing, at first white-eyed, the frightening
mountain gods until they knew those gods
had waited just for them. slowly then they wove
sun, mountain, serpent, eagle, moon
into familiar tapestries of awe and learned
the runes of power and control; aztec, toltec, mixtec,
sioux, inca, blackfeet, navajo, pawnee.

i leave my asiatic window-view
and in my subaru i follow south-
ward their wild experiments, their
searching, their trial and
error wanderings and see their
waiting patience printed every-
where against the sky, their eagle-
feathers everywhere along the great divide,
the spinal ridges of my country.
mine? no. i am the stranger here.
this is indian country
to the bone, the very marrow
of its being. these mountains have the time
and will to wait forever. my little car
coughs slightly at a pass's freezing height
but clings surefooted to the slippery curve.

Before

We are starting on a long journey
We are going north.
The stars will lead us.

We must leave this place now
It has been our home
But now we must leave it
and we must go to the north.

It is very exciting. We will have many adventures.
Some will die and we will see new things.
But those who stay here will surely die.

For those who came here can conquer everything
And they will certainly return with
Their loud animals and sudden fire.

Tears flow from us as streams from the hills
Though we shall have many adventures
Tears flow from us as streams from the hills
As the tears of rain from the black cloud.

The red earth has been disgraced by our blood.
Those who came here to conquer were not gods.
Their red blood ran too, and has poisoned our earth.

Brothers who are staying we pray to you
Do not work this horrible red earth.
We pray to you follow after us.
Come after us to the north.

We will have many adventures there.
It will be very exciting.

C. Columbus — A Comparison

Poet is like C. Columbus
putty face all smile
buttonhook of eye
phony of phonies
dream of prevailing
moonbound on a Vespa
to Isabel's amaze
and Ferdinand's
wide-open greed.

From Genoa to Lisbon
on a pogo stick comes C., son-
of-a-seacook who
woos and wins Lord Lally-
palooza's datter with
a rubber smile, a hand-
cleaned ruff and really
silly day-dream; I love
a travelling man. C. loved

his brother and would make
him king of Cloud Cuckoo
land, ten thousand
Caribs at his brother's beck. But what
a sailor, C.! Steering between
nightmare and Bermuda, watch
in hand timing his will
beyond its final gasp to the
three minute mile and faint

across the finish to awake
in Cipangu while thousands
storm the field, tear up
the goalposts and he, the fool,
returns another route dangerously

further north, to everyone's dismay
(near mutiny again of course) but C. prevails
and thus discovers the prevailing winds
blow east, toward home, reward,
the day-dream done, the night dream waiting now.

Columbus and the Gatsby Group

When the house strained to take off from East
Egg to begin its long historic flight,
Daisy's pleated dress rippling, fluttering,
and the pongee curtains in the long

white windows whipping in the east wind
like pale flags in that rose-colored space,
the mainsail suddenly caught and billowing and
filling out we were all borne up, the balloon

suddenly unanchored, a picture groaning slightly on
the wall; I knew at once how perfect
the trip would be and that our Captain, Christopher, bending
to Daisy's murmur and her look, excluding all but him,

could safely leave the wheel on automatic pilot
to the Azores; we, knowing this, rejoiced. Shoreless
the seas lapped, and now beyond all islands we
were beyond all storms, for Columbus simply sailed

right over them, pointing out the would-be dangerous
                              thunderheads.
He promised that *Japon* was imminent (just beyond the wild
                              Bermoothes
coming up) and then, he said, he planned the moon and
certain stars. The godblown breeze blew notes along our

skins, made even more music of Daisy's pleats opening and
closing, Jordan's cotton flutter, and the whipping curtains.
Our balloon on course we floated, too, inside it, to and from
each other in fine exciting side trips, but Tom

Buchanan crossed the room and that loud boom resounded
as he slammed the long French windows closed and the
                              caught wind
died and the curtains and the rugs and all of us ballooned
gently to the floor and the picture stopped its soft groaning

on the wall. The voyage was over but this was all right. Bearable.
We were used to it. We could stand things as they must be.
We wept, yes. Still we could stand things as they were. But
what of Christopher? What of our Captain, Christopher? He
was real!

Night Dreams

-1-

the bull again by night
Lyon; led in by an acquaintance
a man I met in Skyros
(where Achilles hid from the draft)
who emptied the island
for a book (Univ. S. Cal.)
on economics, a textbook.
And Skyros would make
pix but had little to say about
Econ. unless a very primit.
book. I wondered. Enter with bull
and I warning all
Lyon
to beware beware but they sure
he has bull control
I hide I hide hoping it
not subject to my wish;
bull spared me
with a warning, and my son.

-2-

Cracking, it is cracking
like a tree taken in winds
taken in winds or a
thanksgiving nut by a child
with great crackers
and no one to weep
but myself who, Lyon,
never believed it was real
but do now; cracking,
but not a child here
or even a wind.

I can't believe it
that ministers are soft and their
smiles; anything formal;
Lyon, that if you make the effort you'll
or say write a book
                    improve
it always seemed backward
you were no good to start
and got worse
but you believed in love
right up till the
and he heard his ex had
said bad things about
him in bed, bad;
Agammemnon had the right idea
kick them both in the ass
and bawl orders all over
as if you believed yourself
except it's so godamned tiring;
my father used to say
of the grand sunset
being ah'd over
"you can't eat it,"
success as beauty,
all formal things.

Athens

-1-

The gods of the sea
are reduced to selling sponges
on the streets of sea-facing Athens

and I to waiting
in a hotel room
with a wily fly

who has become

mon ami.

-2-

Going out at last
I picked up on Syntagma
a Japanese girl
          so beautiful
you could carve her only out of
          solid light-brown
Delian alabaster
putting onyx for the eyes
          and so quiet

she must be a bride.
But I got drunk
and shocked her
with modern American
poetry and the wildness
of my laughter.

Walking by the Aegean
I wrote a poem
with no pen or pencil handy
and now cannot recall anything
about it except its quality.

My language,
one with my form,
was unearthly
and splendor leaked from it
like moonlight and a man
singing of moonlight
among tigers,

the only time I have caught
the true curve
of beauty.

poet and child at the piraeus

he took me through the naked-kouroi room
where all the lovely boys stood straight and stiff
like soldiers of a pharaoh   their eyes
forever stricken with infinity.

he pointed out the awesome beauty of
their genitals, nates and their hips,
subjects i had never concentrated
on before;   i was a boy of twelve.

much to note, he said; the scrotal wrinkles,
for example, contrasting with the textured
grain of thigh as smooth as honey looks;
and prepuces were all-important too,

possessed the power to show the inner boy
as graced or graceless through eternity if
beauty did indeed reflect our depths, he said; stand-
ards here are new, he said; your father would agree.

at twelve that night he took me to
the oddest place i'd seen, to meet
a fisherman i'd love, he said; a cafe
at the piraeus jammed with·drunken sailors;

one sailor laughed at him and poked his great round
belly and he giggled i thought foolishly;
but when his friend did not appear
by one he fell as silent as a stone

his sunken eyes like beryl under sea,
and seemed to me beside him in that din
beside the dark aegean, nakeder and
lovelier than a kouros for his grief.

The Mountains

In seconds the small roadside quarrel becomes the
                    real thing.
Two crows in a sudden aerial dogfight try
                    to pick
each other to death. They buzz the mountain
                    lake in
the caw caw caw of hill murder. But the sound
                    falls away,
wings flap away, the ill thing forgotten quick
                    as it began.
In the towering presence of every day, life and death
                    matters
must wait. We go back to our dead dog on the mountain
                    highway.

Danger of Danger/Bermuda

Shark or shade over there
ten yards to the right
hugging this diving rock?
Everyone's like bait in these warm
waters. I have to let my son swim

here though. His mother insists, a fan-
atic on bravery, she watches us
from the beach. I watch him go off
the diving rock, flat as a flounder
splash of butterfish in a swirl of salt.

I mustn't let him see my imagined
shark in the shade, possible for me
and such as me. My only plan is
to really move fast if the shade should
and horror is I can imagine me not.

Old Sculptor/New Love

Tiredness takes him the way passion used to.
His new demon-love, sleep, turns his bones
to lost-wax. After lunch
he lies still as a noon hillside inside her
touching the low relief of dreams.

Meanings waver in this change. Going in
or coming out of sleep a single shoe-skate
in the front hall closet long ago
holds sadness firmly like a big-boned foot.
A boyhood friend looms lifesize in angry walnut
unfinished in the corner, and Miss Sawtell
in the third grade who squeezed his chin
hard enough to change its shape forever
one day when he had whispered
has tapering-fingered hands of gentle alabaster and her
thin translucent neck is bent in pure contrition.

When the tiredness begins the remembered forms
of children, animals, old men
fill him with anxiety
for all the innocent wood he has not shaped,
for his God is implacable
against the formless,
an eternal shaper:
Take thou thy hatchet
and hew the rough-skinned unused lobster buoy
into an honest saint.

Old needs remind his bones each morning but fatigue
soon beats his game and he enters his lovely demon sleep
with the same mid-morning guilt he had for
close-grained Bett at nineteen who gave him his son Robert,
sharp-angled Agnes at forty-five who gave him nothing
from which his courage and his best work grew.

Bonescan — 1982

Patricia went for her semiannual
bonescan today and the weather is on cue
with hail driving against her new aluminum shutters
like b.b.'s and
the whole sky turning black as her hair.

A severe thunderstorm has been foretold
but I am, I believe, not terribly apprehensive
waiting here at home in my room with
the three great uncurtained French windows,
lightning flashing in them every second
like big guns in the distance. I am made
for crisis, like Napoleon's General Murat
I come up to normal in the thick of things,
cool and poised, ready. Few know this about me
and sometimes it's not true

but now the cooler I seem to get the darker and windier
the day becomes, the hail now slashing at the house
like an avenging sword. The oak is groaning,
bends back each way further than I've ever seen it,
looks as if it will rid itself of its encircling poison-
ivy, tear it off by main force, a Jason's wild princess
tearing at her wedding present from Medea or that
                              poor Nessus —
somebody said, around 1950 I think, that a neurosis was
                              harder to get
rid of than a Nessian shirt, even than one's own skin.

The thickening storm is telling us that need shapes answers.
Ivy finds its victim oak and vice versa. I'm a pro tem
                              Murat out
of terror, though perhaps for lesser storms than this. Each
                              to his
own neurosis, dear to him, a clinger. I read somewhere that
the West needs cancer to help control its monstrous pride.

The storm is teaching Western depth psychology, secular
                                    and circular,
with even Freud's negative exception
to prove it's right: *Because we need him, God does not exist.*
                        It seems
impossible but the wind is still increasing. Terrifying now. It's
black as an eclipse inside this thick of things
the whirlwind not foretold.

Priestess

The day I told her who she was and she believed me
we were a seven-sided church on a Greek promontory.

The day she told me the meaning of my fear and I wept
                              and it
left me forever, we were two figures in a myth walking
                     among poplars.

The day we spent in the house on the edge of the Aegean
we were two dolphins waving hello endlessly.

The day she went walking alone and disappeared in a dazzle
                           of sun
around a stand of myrtle we were two white clouds drifting
                    in company.

But the day she painted the picture of herself with streaming
                     yellow hair
driving a red convertible, a terrible thunderstorm blew in,

and the day she decided to stay a month longer in
                        Greece, alone,
was a day of low red tides, mudflats stinking of stranded fish,

and the day she came home with the dead cat in her arms
she was carrying our marriage.

Letter from the Country

Dear Grim, there's nothing much to tell
nothing to do here still but books and movies
cold weather holds, the sky is columbine
and certain trees desert us for the reds

early defectors; the birds too cry war
flee south hysterical and clog the sky;
tomorrow, Rick writes, he goes for his physical
and has high hopes he'll be rejected
for mental reasons; one can only pray;

enclosed another note for Alice that I leave unsealed
for you to read and mail from there;
she's mad if she believes she'll ever find me;
who did she think she was deceiving; a fool?

well, I've said all that before; it must get boring
nothing else much; write soon again, the people here
don't take one in, a stranger.

Sexual Instruction

He invites me to an orgy; he
lectures like a fish in goggles
across the table on how we georgie-
porgies have had the joy trained

out of us — his tongue studies the left
corner of his mouth during his pauses —
"Your senses are systematically bereft
of their potential, your passion has been

drained and they've replaced it with embalming fluid."
His eyes flash angrily behind his metal
rims and he goes on: "The mind boggles
at what you take as gospel; the petal

of soul will die inside such armor; life-in-
death; beauty-blind." He sighs, points to
his eyes. "You're beauty-blind," he shouts: "a blue druid!"
I accept the invitation to the orgy.

There, naked, he keeps his glasses on; it
makes him look as if he had his socks on; his tongue
studies his mouth's edge; critical bee among dubious
flowers giving them all okays though none are earned.

I take my shoes and glasses off and socks but
my armor won't budge. I charge about, greaved,
metalled, helmeted and plumed; and spurned. What
can dubious flowers do to help a blue druid? I grieve

openly but they are nohow interested in my kind
of person or problem. Two months later I meet my
present wife. Our passion is a wind to put it mildly;
whirlwind, but slow to grow. It takes a month to kiss

her. Have hardly ever seen her naked yet, four kids
and twenty years later; but the idea alone inflames me still.

not remembering

is like almost hearing
flash, no thunder,
only the will to hear;

is often dangerous,
a photo of Uncle Sancto's
lap and ruby lips,
his broken fingernail
an agony of cigarsmoke,
his gift to you
of the sharp clear picture (small
tic of right eye, lifelong terror
of closeness)
on the bureau
in the hiding place from yourself
he made inside you;

is a deerlike creature suddenly met
with two small balsams for his horns
the top of each departing bound
a willed act
to come down
not fly.

remembering

not the fact of the thin ten-dollar whore's presence
in their sacred bedroom but her face on seeing the
quilted bed-canopy, the closetful of clothes, Mary's
shoes. she knelt down and counted them as if she were
praying to herself. "Jesus Christ," she said at last,
"fifty two pairs!" and her sudden eyes turned panic
at the error of her ways.

she wanted to try on one of Mary's dresses. his skin
crawls remembering he wouldn't let her, remembering she
wouldn't make love to him after that even for fifty. why did
he want to? he did though. she looked like Mary. same
kind of frame, same hips, same legs. but why didn't he
let her try the dress on? keep the fucking thing for
Christ's sweet sake? he played it backwards.

Mary would have thought she left it someplace. she was
always losing clothes, forgetting what she owned, saying
"i haven't got a single decent skirt," when she had ten.
later he could have told Mary he could remember she'd got
some spots on that particular dress, that he was certain
it'd been taken to the cleaner's months before. it might
have saved the young whore's face with herself getting
a dress like that for free. it might just have made her
passionate as hell. she looked like Mary even in the face
around the eyes so what sin would that have been for Christ's
sweet sake.

Anger, Long-tempered, Years Later

How I ran for Grindle on that icy
indoor-outdoor wooden track in upper Maine.
He had those stopwatch eyes, that click-on smile
that said: "I love him"   "all heart"   "he never quits."

I won Exeter and I won Andover and I won Choate for him
and tied the Lower Maine record for the mile
against Tufts Freshmen. Grindle's click-on
smile turned permanent. I danced from cloud to

peak to cloud and bulldog linesmen on the
football team gave me their quick front
teeth and flag of hand. But then one weekend
down at Stowe, Vermont, I got on skis, though

Grindle had said and more than once, "No
skiing and no skating and don't forget that.
Don't forget." But I forgot or something. I smashed
my knee and never ran again. Flexion gone, a

cut-through cartilage. Oh, I tried. I was absurd,
could only gallop now. He watched me trying but
only from a distance. He never spoke to me again,
never wrote a note saying "I told you so," or "We could've

beat in the Olympics, you asshole, you featherbrain
pile of galloping horsemeat." Rage. Anything. I needed
help. Afterward for years I ran for you smoothly
like fleeing light, oh Grindle, like insane hope oh Timer

whose eyes loved my thunder on the frozen wood but whose
silly ticking mind could not, speed dead, pray for my
                    endurance to survive.

The Gift

"I never promised you a rowboat."
My father actually said that line.
He said it decades ago. He said it

on my ninth birthday when I cried
and sulked thinking he *had* promised
me one. God alone knows how I

came by such a thought. Pa simply didn't
believe in such big gifts. None of us
even had a bike though we were far

from poor. Eleven kids. And so I stole
the rowboats of the lobster men as they
lay sleeping in the long hot Marshfield,

Massachusetts afternoons of summer, dreaming
of lobster pots as firmly fully packed
as boiled, red lobster claws. I liked

John Greenleaf's boat the best, oars
always in it, the lightest. Out our channel
on the ebb I'd shoot, into the calm of Cape

Cod Bay. What things I saw! A silver
horse in ten clear yards of water; the
great rust freckles on a sunken Checker

Taxi. Fins were everywhere; wise
dolphins circled me and shining
baked clay starfish moved in a glazed

descending measure. All was weaving waving
formal pattern, designed at the antipodes where
winds blew ribs and ripples in shell and sand

in endless art. Provincetown beckoned. It
looked so near. I'd want to try it every time.
And once I did. It was dark before

I turned back and dark as well when I
came up the channel. Mr. Greenleaf
was waiting on the muddy shore with folded

arms, his rubber boots colossal. But what
he said was: "Steal it a little earlier after
this, if you don't mind, Leonard. I go out at dark now."

Whistle and Call/Mexico

The knife-sharpener's two-noted whistle and his call are
sweet as the tootle of my wife's recorder from her
rooftop study in this morning's sun-drenched mist.
Knives. Knives.

Egrets swoop over and roost in two distant pine trees.
A far-off car churns soft as the off-white Essex of
my sister's boyfriend outside our house forever

every night at midnight, goodnight oh goodnight. This morning
the light's as creamy as my mother's velvet party dress or
pa's white flannels that he kept creased sharp enough
to cut yourself on.

Three: Back Ways In

Envy's Stinging

The sun slowly stunned us. Over 100 F.
in that thin frazzled shade for fifteen days.
It scrambled our brains, dried out our
hearts and scorched our treeless grass and blistered
the new siding on the house

until one afternoon just after 3 o'clock
we fled the fifty miles to our nearest woods
barely knowing what we hoped for there
and found the woods had known exactly
what to do.

Using the awful sun against itself they'd
formed cathedral shades we'd never seen before,
green wonders, numberless. An oak was
eye-shade green, an apple all green-eyed,
a dark ravine was olive and an ash was olive-
drab. All ocean as we walked was there, the bronze
Pacific dominating perhaps among low-growing bushes
but the Atlantic rolled there too
in barrel-vaulted treeheads in a north green wind
at the forest's center.

And at the forest's center three gray-green birds
on glaucous-honeysuckle sang,
a clerestory choir, of love of love
and a spring-green elm stood vast as the aurora
in a citrine mood while birches in their turqoise
camouflage shivered far more than sun could think
was right and the three gray-green birds sang without stop
from their choir.

Cool as wet fern we felt we could not leave now, ever.
But we couldn't plant ourselves or fly
and so instead we lay upon a bed of moss
to hidden-dark for green to even show
and let our envy for all shadow
caw our passion out
like emerald parrots.

common hiding place

a miracle, a horror or a wonder can,
as well as a purloined letter,
hide within the shell of everydayness.
unnoted, inside its double valves you find:

a blue eye reflected in two mirrors to a black
infinitude; kangaroo night leaping in terror
before the lion light; passion of the passion-
flower under the sun's blind wants;

grief a book to learn;
night-heart, day-reason; lost love
of self found whole in real love's looking-
glass; art's front reflecting, reflecting;

the arts of night; mind pacing
its cage of never-knowing; the
eternal presence of the cruel; the
reassuring laughter in all shade.

Yes,

the white estrellas at Las Casas were magnificent;
          red meadow
and noon-time stars, and the wild, blood-
          streaked mums
waiting in silence; the short-stemmed sun
          was fat
with shade; a common cardinal whirred up up up
          from the
crimson cover along the border of the red-
          haired corn.

Did you signal, beckon me as we picked the wild-
          flowers?
Was I slow? What could I give you? Listen, it is
          better
without touch, better to just sit in each other's
          hearts,
fragrant, vased, fresh. Sun kisses estrella and
          moves on.

The planned furrow's dark and wormful, dull with
          love of
rusting vegetables. Far love is much better; we can
          be like
two blood-red birds racing up up up to burst
          together
into that thin air crammed with figs and fat
          promises
chameleons search for endlessly, gorge them-
          selves on.

When They Grow Close Together

Tall trees, ash, beech, joyfully
join heads in small breezes
and branches talk
with their hands;
leaves spin like
silver words, ex-
cited; heads
in a gust
bend backward
like dancers
their branches
palms up like
friends getting
the point of the
story; leaves shine
like laughter,
"oh, god, that's marvelous,"
then heads come
together again.

In a high wind
they join in grief,
leaves tearing
branches groaning
rended; cracking;
the huge torsos sway
first side to side
then from their roots
way way over
way way back
together again
like tall Jews remembering,
their cries drawn from them,
"It's good to see you. Thank
God you're here at this time."

To Market

This chilly early morning in our mountain town
a clubfoot woman, barefoot, wearing a purple skirt
with orange hem and carrying some small burden in
her blue rebozo, descends, just before the sun has

reached it, the steep and sharp-stoned path that leads
into our cobbled street on the town's north edge.
She walks in breakneck iambs, seen not heard, but
felt, as jolts, as though she carried us

in all that pounding haste. A boy in white is peeing
at the wall that holds the sloping mesquite grove
above our street; he turns his head to watch her; two
other shivering boys look up from marbles and

we all smile to see a pinkfaced footbound piglet
peeping out, resigned, even content, inside her
blue rebozo as she posts on past us down
our curving street, passing beyond us. Suddenly

we see, yawning before her (first of the day) a torrent
of sunlight that, pouring like a mountain stream
between two gaps — one in our hills and one between
our close-built houses — makes a tremendous puddle, a

deep pond of light, into which she plunges, up to her
middle, over her head and disappears in total dazzle
on her way to market, to market. We zip up, finish our
marbles, and, warmer already, hobble off into the
                              drowning day.

Wonder

If you were an Arm with an Eye
and a Nose, you'd (objective, fresh-viewing)
soon know how strange we are.

Here for what reason? Who brought us,
Arm? It's weird. I mean brought all
of us, moss-green cockatoos, silk-

screen junkos, beavers and eager
snakes, sniffing, hugging the
ground like brokers on the traces

of a runaway ticker? And then
mosquitoes, for the love of God, Arm!
Scorpions, swift as rats, rabbits screaming

like murdered babies and jumping-jack
sun, up-down. Why these, Arm? Smell how strange.
Love's altar just where Yeats, among others, put it.

And worse — Beauty! Why this, why *this*, Arm?
Fields on fields of silver bells pure as
stopped sunlight and then the blinding yellow

flowers, hammered petal-thin right in the
fields by smiths of gold, in worship, yet.
And if you were not an Arm with an Eye

and a Nose but were a Hand with an Ear, you'd
hear how strange the bees, Hand, like hungry
violins playing up a storm over the drowning

orchard and meaning every note and every pause —
meaning drum of hunger, hum of work, horn of mystery,
strings of love, throat of war, horn of silence.

And if, Hand, you heard a single nightingale
in Greece or England, say, and having no eyes to weep
with, then, perhaps, you might really hear

(caught in this Beauty like quicksand, like children
in amber, beached listening angels)
how utterly strange we are, how weird, Hand.

Whole Saler

i been in vanilla beans this week
up to my ears and in moist-mocha
recently up to the eyes; bought three
chockful gloriettas of steaming

cabooch and mucho corny chowder ingreds,
with small bear-beans, black-eyed boomquats,
some winterwipple and musical pears. i
deal in futures only. martha likes them.

i deal in snow-sugar futures, web-sugar futures,
darning needle brownsalt and i bought two doz.
redrockcandy jetties and a gross of licorice
wirelesses off hatteras for rich nine-year-

olds; *semper paratus*, martha always says; hectare of
seedcake soaked in three cloy of hymettus honey and
transportation for it, 30 wagons w/beer-colored
horses, what's to worry, i can always use them,

martha says. grapes are a glut so i
buy a glut all-concord. yes, indeed, the vanilla
beans were winged, soared (a local frost) i made a killing,
so next week will surely go to maple-sugar crystal-tree,

molasses-mull, cinnamon-pull and chimney-cream; sweets.
martha was poor and likes them best.

Brother Lax,

once an astronomer, now sees Prime Number
in the daisy field of night as
marking footpaths through Orion
with signposts so irregularly placed
that even God could have forgotten
these back ways in.

He guards his Order's huckleberries like
a shepherd, discovers each hiding redness
from his hilltop perch. Responsible
for peaches too
he knows when flush
or yellow will shine through
as sure as when the blush
on his shy cheeks will come
in company with his fellow monks
if he should speak, so
no peach falls is dashed.

Brother Lax, in love
with fields and orchards
down here, up there
what matter
long as they have hidden paths
and shine.

Hard Questions to Some Animals, with Answers

Why do you nibble and pray and
nibble all over the clover, rabbit?

      "Clover is the sun."

Why do you eat the high-jumping eland and
why do you eat the almost-flying eland, great cat?

      "Eland is the sun."

Why, dog, do you look at me as though I were
God? Why do your eyes follow me with a
saint-like adoration? *You* know that *I*
know you're hardly spiritual, that you
concentrate on food almost to the total
exclusion of everything else.

      "Food is the sun."

The sun! The sun! Can't you answer with anything
else? Do you think the sun is God? That God is a total
materialist? Does he mean nothing more to you than
food? Well, answer me. All of you. Is the food-giving
sun God?

      "No. The sun is a messenger."

A messenger? A messenger? And what is its so holy
message then? Eat? Go thou and eat?

      "Oh, no. Be full."

Be full? That's the messenger's message from
God? That's *it?* That's the whole thing? Be full?

      "No. Also, be not empty."

Ode to Light

-1-

I lie here
at the bottom
of night
like a trout
and I know
your secret, Light.

-2-

First, master of image, I will tell of your
soon-coming dawn, reflect how still once more
your elephants of broken silk will come massing
in our corners, the color of laughing as your crowny pikes,

rose-gold, ascend the stage and the wild dance of day begins
from the horizon. Smooth fleer on all roads now you
                         will flood
our diamond globe with massive flowering and paint
                         again the
egret's royal maneuvers and his hopes. Tripping among

pools of shadow, model of all laughter, Clown, bouncing,
                         toppling
off the roof of heaven, off the wall and through my window,
bluebird, through my window in your invisible
world-suit, splitting in two at tree trunks, expression-

less, clown-cheek fiery, shattering among a million leaves,
mocking the timid wind his roaring wholeness, his silly groans,
with tripping mottles, turning wind-sighs to laughter, to seen
arpeggios from your vast bag of counterpoint, your infinite

music-box of shade. Armies of starlings will kiss you open-
mouthed, and the nightingale who has learned to tell your
beauty
back in sound, and does, from her tree, to hold you, try to
hold you,
wild visitor, when, at each day's end you turn twirling

your peacock cape of twilight, aster-lined, to leave us.
Moctezuma
trembled like the nightingale and kept his singers up all
night for
he could well imagine a king-caused dark forever. What can be
imaged can be so. You, juggler of reflection, taught him that.

-3-

But your secret; you travel unenchanted
through the darkness; I see you, clear as day,
holding your breath as you shuttle, bored
as time through space, look straight ahead
not right or left. Until you reach us. Then,
click, we turn you on and then you flood us
with your self, hold nothing back. I see you,
arriving, breathe again. Home. House that sunlight
built. You love the earth. You love us. Secret clear
as day.

-4-

Our heads are small suns, moon-
round; thought is ray-like, all-flooding
reflective, refractive, quick as shadow,
mimetic as shadow, vault of laughter. Our
eyes see seven hues, all you bring, the
sum of the transparent, and you
are emperor here, creator of all
that is seen, seen through; creator of
we who see you and our palaces.

Purloined Answer
are you an envoy?
Can we take your
single-minded
travelling
as a sign?

Beloved Light
none here laugh at
Moctezuma
now. En-
force your
laughter,
teach us to live in
opalescent
castle, all
window open
all wall a
see-through
walk-through
glistening-always
upstairs
downstairs
through the dark night's
dangers.

in the window of knowing

i know, Lord, i have awe of You hiding in me
as if it were a grievous matter. Musk Of The Frozen
Himalayas In Rose, know that i tremble in my belly
at You. though they hold their smiling Logic up

and swing its foolish grin before us like
an incense pot to still our awful terror of Thee
and loose our hidden grasp upon Thee, Royal
Palm Of Time i am glued against the duty of Your Body.

they need to kill us, Lord, for eternity. last
night that dr. hummingbird with his gigantic sweet-
ness needle lulled me and softened me and when i
tried to sing to You, oh Violet In Music Like

Water, oh Pterodactyl Of The Hidden Moon, my notes
froze in my throat, my clutching fingers slid off the side
of heaven's flank and i heard Your Voice inside
me far off as in a tomb. they bury You. o blast

them with an unheard note, Musk Of Small Snow Roar-
ing In The Andes, Terrible Hand In The Window Of
Knowing, blow out past every inwardness oh Pterodactyl
Of The Hidden Sun and let, oh Lord, Thy Kingdom Come.

Near Damascus

In that mysterious event
first hands break into feeling
and then along the skin
the million-year-old eyes,
numberless, open
like pond lilies;

next the heart breaks into blossom
as if into fire;

then last, the day-closed flower of grief
breaks into metaphorless flame
and is consumed,
leaving no slightest trace
as if it had not been
nor even been imagined.

The poems in this book are printed in 11 point California Bold type, on 70 pound Sundance Bright White text. The cover stock is 10 point Cast Coated Cover and the fly sheet is 80 pound Legendry Indigo text. Of an initial printing of 1000, 50 have been numbered and signed by the author.